The Age of the Lily,
Sophia, The Wisdom of God—
The Spirit of Truth, the Spirit of Fusion:
Spirit of His Spirit, Love of His Love,
by Gabriele

*The Eternal Word,
the One God, the Free Spirit,
speaks through Gabriele,
as through all the prophets of God—
Abraham, Job, Moses, Elijah, Isaiah,
Jesus of Nazareth,
the Christ of God*

The Age of the Lily,

Sophia, The Wisdom of God—
The Spirit of Truth, the Spirit of Fusion:

Spirit of His Spirit,
Love of His Love

Gabriele,
The teaching prophetess and
emissary of God in our time

Gabriele
Publishing House

*"The Age of the Lily,
Sophia, The Wisdom of God—
The Spirit of Truth, the Spirit of Fusion:
Spirit of His Spirit, Love of His Love"*

1st Edition, December 2023
© Gabriele-Verlag Das Wort GmbH
Max-Braun-Str. 2, 97828 Marktheidenfeld
www.gabriele-verlag.com
www.gabriele-publishing-house.com

Translated from the original German title:

„Das Lilienzeitalter
Sophia, die Weisheit Gottes – Der Geist der Wahrheit,
der Geist der Fusion:
Geist aus Seinem Geiste, Liebe aus Seiner Liebe"

The German edition is the work of reference
for all questions regarding the meaning of the contents.

All rights reserved

Order No. S190TBEN

All decorative letters: © Gabriele-Verlag Das Wort

Printed by: KlarDruck GmbH, Marktheidenfeld, Germany

ISBN 978-3-96446-423-1

The Age of the Lily,
Sophia, The Wisdom of God—
The Spirit of Truth, the Spirit of Fusion:
Spirit of His Spirit,
Love of His Love

Time passes, but many things remain present.

Nearly five decades ago, I, Gabriele, was called by the eternal All-One God to be the prophetess of God.

The Cherub of His divine Wisdom trained me, so that I serve the Eternal Kingdom, the Kingdom of God, as prophetess. How that took place and what became of it, has been passed on in several divine revelations.

My "yes" to the Eternal, to the almighty Father-Mother-Being, became the task to fulfill and to give the divine-prophetic word, which has now been revealed in this world for nearly five decades and, via radio, television and other media, reaches ever more people, and beyond that, also the souls in the soul realms.

After some time of spiritual-divine schoolings, of training to be the prophetess of the eternal All-One, the *I Am the I Am* briefly, and without ifs and buts, revealed itself and disclosed to me my spiritual-divine origin in its depth.

As I grew into the prophetic task by way of the schoolings more and more, I directed a great request to the eternal All-One, for His eternal, primordially holy word now began to spread and appealed greatly to more and more listeners. My request was: *Eternal All-One, please conceal from the public the depth of my origin from the Kingdom of God.*

For years, it was kept this way, although every now and then my spiritual-divine origin was touched upon in a general way in many a revelation of God from the kingdom of the eternal Being. From decade to decade, it became ever clearer from where the eternal word comes. During the last decade, the "from where the eternal word comes" was far more directly pointed out and can now no longer be concealed by me, Gabriele.

The eternal All-One wanted and now wants it this way, since, He, the Spirit of truth, had and still has plans for the human being, Gabriele, in order to make manifest the deep meaning of His words: *My daughter.*

It was difficult for me to accept this statement for a long time, because I was once a shy girl who had to survive the difficult time of the Second World War with her mother and grandmother at her side; father was in the war. My grandmother struggled every day for food, so that we, mother, child and grandmother, had food to eat. Grandmother, once a trained cook, had lots of experience in making something more out of little food.

Thus, I was a shy girl and in later years a very reserved young woman, even though my temperament had its roots and its expression. During the following decades, my life as a married woman proceeded as in other marriages. Life had its highs and lows.

Then my life took an unforeseeable turn. I said "yes" to the eternal All-One and had to adjust completely, in order to live up to the "yes" to Him. Now, my further path of life was shaped by the divine schoolings through my spiritual teacher, Brother Emanuel.

During these divine and intense schoolings, every now and then my spiritual teacher let me look into the Eternal Kingdom. I beheld the beauty, the unity and the oneness of the divine, of the heavenly beings.

I beheld the heavenly buildings, the gardens and landscapes, heavenly nature and the most diverse species of animals and the becoming and being in the four planes of development to the filiation of God. I looked into the primordial work of creation of the four powers of creating and into the three attributes of the Father-Mother-Being, the filiation attributes. More and more, I, Gabriele, found my way into the primordial eternal law of love for God and neighbor.

Dear fellow people, that is why, in myself, I rebel against all the debasements that are imposed on the word "God." Although God is the Spirit of life, He is demeaned by many, very many people in the western world, for example, with exclamations like: "Oh God, oh God!" or "Oh, dear God!" or "God damn it!" or with the casually and indifferently spoken: "Greetings in God," etc.

Every country has its corresponding disparagement, which seems like a cudgel to me, with which one simply wants to beat upon God, who is the love and truth. This language of beating against God is often used by the people, including church believers and by church and state powers, as well, especially in connection with the abuse of the words "Christian values" and other expressions of discrimination.

To me, God is the Spirit of truth, the Spirit of life, the Spirit of the love for God and neighbor.

The one who has neither respect nor reverence for the mighty Spirit of life cannot understand me when I write:

God is the Spirit of truth, the Spirit of life, who is omnipresent and flows and flows and flows. He flows through all universes; He flows through the material universe. He shines in all the suns and planets.

God, the omnipresent streaming Being, is the infinite Light-Ether, which is the luminosity of infinity. The Spirit of infinity flows through every human being. The Spirit of truth flows and touches the negativity in the human being only briefly and without value judgment, in order to draw his attention to what he could remedy.

The Spirit of truth streams through infinity without interruption. The Spirit of truth is the Spirit of fusion, about which we will still read and hear.

I repeat: No matter what we people call the Spirit of God—He is the flowing Spirit, the All-Law of infinity.

The institutional ecclesiastical sorry effort knows nothing of all this and is therefore completely in the dark, also in terms of the content of the word "God," who is depicted by the churches as a far distant being and, if possible, as an old man who punishes sins and condemns people according to their fall into sin. In reality, such a "god" does not exist.

In the religions, many things are particularly contrived, so that people fear "god." This "god" is the "god" invented by the guild of priests, the idolatrous god, who enslaves people with punishment, hell and damnation, and also with cults, dogmas and the like.

In all of infinity, there is no entity called "god." God is the All-power, the All-Law, the Spirit of truth, the Spirit of life.

As already mentioned: The primordial eternal law, the All-Law, which we, in the western world, so profanely call "God," streams throughout all universes, every rate of vibration, every frequency, every form, every object, everything, all of matter, infinity.

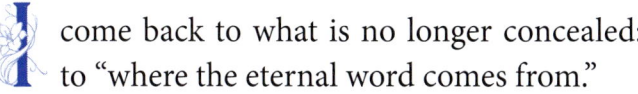 come back to what is no longer concealed: to "where the eternal word comes from."

Now, after nearly five decades, the Eternal reveals in the word of His prophetess, Gabriele:

My daughter, I raise the veil, and you report how it was, how it is, what you behold, how the Eternal Kingdom, which is the eternal homeland of all divine beings, developed.

You are still a human being, but your spiritual being comes from the "Let there be," in order to give form to the desire of the fusion, to found the Eternal Kingdom and to have the formation from the infinite Being take place.

And so it was: The core of being of my soul opened more and more, and I behold and report:

Before the creation of Being, before the "Let there be" to the eternal Being, there was solely infinite light, seas of light, also called flowing Light-Ether.

All in all, it is the Spirit of truth, highest vibrating energies, infinite aspects of consciousness of diverse currents of light—light-ethereal.

The Spirit of truth, whom we people in the western world call "God," is the eternal Spirit, the All-flowing life, eternally. The Spirit, the All-Life, knows neither beginning nor end—He is.

To repeat:
Until the creation, until the "Let there be," there were solely inexhaustible, highest vibrating energies of diverse aspects of consciousness, inexhaustible, infinite seas of light, spirit of His Spirit, eternal light, Light-Ether.

Dear fellow people, we are talking here about the truth from dimensions that are not comprehensible with the cognitive possibilities of our alleged three dimensions—if they are three dimensions at all. That is the truth of it!

Our eye sees only the dense substance, the shadow, which we human beings call matter. Matter is nothing other than transformed-down primordial substance, transformed down from the Light-Ether, from the Spirit, from the primordial light of infinity.

Everything that concerns the further dimensions can be rendered with our language only in an allusive way. Regardless of how I express it and pass it on in the three dimensions—everything is based on the eternal Spirit, on the primordial eternal All-Law, which is the Spirit of truth.

From the All-Law, from the Spirit of truth to the fusion, emerged the fine-material, forming Eternal Kingdom, which is seven-dimensional. All forms, colors, tones and sounds, all divine beings, called spirit beings, are fine-material, that is, light-ethereal, spirit of His Spirit. Also all forms and colors of the endless gardens and their design, the dwellings, as well as the innumerable animal species and not lastly, the nation of children in unity with the Father-Mother-Being are light-ethereal and spirit of His Spirit that became form, love of His Love, seven-dimensional.

The eternally flowing Spirit is the carrier substance of all fine-material forms, as well as of the Eternal Kingdom and of all cosmoses, including the material cosmos.

The eternally flowing Spirit is the primordial law that we humans in the western world call "God."

Everything, but absolutely everything, is consciousness, which, according to its state of consciousness, expresses itself in forms, colors, fragrances and sounds, and this, in all of infinity.

All of what I have only briefly indicated here was preceded by a mighty cosmic fusion, by way of the Spirit of truth to the "Let there be."

The fusion was the desire and the will of the competencies of the bearers of consciousness of the infinite seas of light, the "Let there be." It drew and created and unfolded itself into seven-dimensional forms and colors—the becoming of the light-ethereal Eternal Kingdom.

Everything that we human beings see, and do not see, is energetic Light-Ether, ether atoms of light that create and create; it is forming life, that, which the infinite fusion inherently contains:

Light-ethereal waves upon waves of light, energetic seas of light and their gradual melding into cosmic unity, into the "Let there be," into the drawing and creating Being.

I, Gabriele, can only pass on this unique event with three-dimensional words, since I am among human beings as a human being.

The Cherub of eternal Wisdom gave a revelation about the nature of the seas of light and about the convergence of these seas of light, in which he pictorially reflected the cosmic events.

In this context, he spoke of "ethereal matrixes," which formed into a kind of rhythmic waves, with the confluence of the seven seas of light.

With the repeated superimposition of the currents of light-ethereal waves, so-called "water images" emerged.

The Cherub of the eternal Wisdom of the Being called what became apparent from the confluence of the light-ethereal waves: "matrix images."

Before the mighty event of the "Let there be," there were several attempts at this.

However, four drawing and creating seas of infinitely flowing light had similar polarities. The confluence of these light-ethereal waves upon waves, floods of light from four largely equally vibrating energies of consciousness, produced no success—for they were polarities of a similar structure, even of the same consciousness, the same wavelength—until a fifth light-ethereal sea of currents of consciousness flowed in, which contained within three sea surges of light-ethereal consciousness, and signaled its intention.

It may all sound mundane, but I can merely convey the whole thing with three-dimensional words.

The fifth mighty consciousness, with three vast sea currents of light—light-ethereal energies of a magnitude that surpassed all four equally vibrating sea surges of light together—is the Spirit of truth, which flowed into the four energetic drawing and creating sea surges and revealed his intention.

As already mentioned: The fifth consciousness, with the three gigantic energy currents, drew attention to itself and its intention with the flooding of light.

Through the corresponding influx of waves upon waves, pictorial forms emerged—I would like to call them, as stated, water images.

The fifth consciousness is the Spirit of truth to the "Let there be," the Creator for the forming life.

I repeat: With the influx of light, with infinite ethereal sea surges of light from the fifth mighty consciousness, the plan for the "Let there be" became clear.

The desire and the will of the fifth light-ethereal bearer of consciousness of three ethereal seas of light was to create an infinite eternal kingdom with beings and kingdoms of nature in manifold colors, forms, fragrances and sounds, of course, fine-material, whereby the indicated sounds revealed the communicative interaction of all the forms of life.

The inexhaustible ethereal currents indicated that, to this, the other four gigantic bearers of consciousness were significant, the owners of the four drawing and creating energetic seas of light.

After unimaginable, manifold confluences of energies in matrix-like formations, the bearers of the four and of the three different light-ethereal sea currents observed the flare of the "Let there be."

I find no words other than "gigantic" and "unique" for the merging of these mighty seven cosmic, ethereal energies upon energies.

When the five competencies of the seven seas of light were in agreement, the melding began toward absolute unity, toward the all-permeating cosmic "Let there be." In mighty cycles, they decided to found the Eternal Kingdom and to give themselves form.

The fusion, the melding into absolute unity, brought forth the mighty Being into the "Let there be," the Eternal Kingdom—ultimately, the forming life, the absolute Being. To this powerful, energetic, unique fusion, the vernacular would say: Everything from one source, to the "Let there be."

The infinite currents of light-ethereal seas—called fusion in their absolute melding—are the Spirit, which we in the western world call "God."

For better understanding, let it be repeated again: The melding of seven light-ethereal seas is the Spirit, which has within the light-ethereal formation through the fusion.

The mighty "Let there be" is the All-Spirit, the infinite law of the eternal Being, the love of God. The eternal truth is the Spirit of fusion and therefore, the light-ethereal forming life, spirit of His Spirit, love of His Love.

The core in the fusion is also—seen as the root—the Spirit to the forming life, the Spirit of Kindness, Love and Meekness, of Order, of Will, of Wisdom and of Earnestness.

Just as a tree, a shrub, a flower emerges from a seed, from a kernel, thus, from the mighty fusion, a light-ethereal, fine-material life developed that became form, spirit of the Spirit, of the eternally flowing life.

From the infinite seas of light, the fusion, the core to the "Let there be," the All-creation entity, the sovereign entity, the Father-Mother-Principle, accepted the Being that became form.

In the further mighty course of creation from the core of the fusion, the powers of drawing and creating gave themselves forming life, the entity from the "Let there be," according to their competence.

Just as the crown of a mighty tree gives off its seeds, its kernels, in the same way, according to their competence, entities flowed out of the "Let there be," from the seven infinite streams of the Being.

The core, the fusion, bears the consciousness of giving and receiving of the first dual units: Cherubim and Seraphim, unity principles from the Spirit of the fusion.

Furthermore, the Sanctum is in the origin, it is the creation of the Creator, the Father-Mother-Being. The Sanctum, the central core for the All-Being, is the center of the seven times seven infinitely flowing ethereal energies of consciousness, which were called seas of light or surges of light before the fusion. Seven basic ethereal currents flow to each other and into each other. It is the Spirit of unity and the root of the fusion to the light-ethereal formation. Infinite currents and the potentiating of self takes place in the mighty center of the Being, called the Sanctum.

From the mighty "Let there be," flowed the life, the beginning to the formation of the first entities and the beginning of the mighty Eternal Kingdom. The first basic principles for the life are the stock duals, Cherubim and Seraphim.

From the core of the fusion it continued to the "Let there be." A mighty nation developed. Symbolically speaking, this means that the Eternal Kingdom developed from countless seeds and kernels of a mighty tree, from the trunk and from the one root—the Father-Mother-Principle and the seven entity-powers: kernels, like seeds upon seeds, roots upon roots, the mighty kingdom, the Eternal Kingdom.

Coming back again to the Sanctum, the center of the Being:

The Sanctum is the perpetuum mobile of the All-Being of infinity. The core of the fusion is, as stated, comparable to a mighty tree. The Spirit of life is like a root from which flows the forming life. It is the Spirit of infinity that brings forth the fruit and, at the same time, passes on seeds, or kernels.

It is very difficult to convey the "Let there be" in three-dimensional words, but it is solely about understanding, as far as this is possible, that our souls come from infinity, from the Kingdom of the Being, and that infinity is the Spirit of truth who wants His sons and daughters back, for we are spirit of His Spirit and love of His Love, entities, spirit beings of the true life.

Because this is so, with my three-dimensional words, I am trying to give an understanding of our eternal homeland, for the Eternal and the Eternal Kingdom, the eternal Being, are calling for the sons and daughters of the eternal Being.

Dear fellow people, please understand me! I will repeat myself a few more times, because the whole thing, our true life, is so complex, so filled with substance, and of such a multiplicity of life, that repetitions certainly do not elicit boredom, but contribute to a deeper understanding.

I continue: It flows, and I may look into the mighty currents of the eternal Spirit: the homeland, the kingdom of the Father-Mother-Being, the infinite gardens, the animals, the buildings of the brothers and sisters. In all of the infinite kingdom, there are no masters and maidservants, no servitude and no hegemony.

Everything is unity and love. That is the true life, that is the "Let there be," the Spirit of love that gives and gives.

As already written: The densification, called matter, is nothing other than transformed-down Light-Ether, energy condensed into coarse matter. The human being calls his earthly destination matter, but his origin, and thus, his true destination, is and remains the Spirit, the all-flowing and creating Light-Ether, the Spirit of truth, the Spirit of love and love of neighbor, the Spirit, the law of life, which is unity.

The Spirit of truth, the Spirit of fusion, is the Spirit from which we are all spirit of His Spirit, of the infinite Love that flows and flows—and the human being does not realize that he, too, is being permeated!

Science, quantum physics, would have many terms for this, but none of the so-called experts can prove the Spirit that we human beings in the western world call God.

He is. He flows and has no need to reveal Himself to the experts and suggest to them who He is. He is omnipresent, eternally flowing truth, the Spirit.

The Spirit of truth, the true life, gives and gives and points out what we human beings can change—and not how we should regard Him.

The Spirit of truth is autonomous and not dependent.

Every light-ethereal type of atom is autonomous in itself and works according to the principle of communication, sending and receiving, spirit consciousness with spirit consciousness, everything according to the principle: spirit of His Spirit and love of His Love.

Whether it is the material universe, whether it is the finer or fine-material universes, whether it is the planets or the galaxies or other matter—the infinite, primordial eternal Spirit permeates all things. Whether material universe, fine-material or finer-material—every planet, every sun is merely a drop of the eternal Spirit.

If we look into the so-called night sky, then we believe that it would be dark between the planets. But there is no darkness in all of infinity. The darkness that we think we see is, in reality, filled with the Spirit, with the light that flows through infinity, and thus, also in our three dimensions.

A brother was asked to contribute several aspects and statements from science to these explanations. According to his consciousness, he put together several things:

Science cannot grasp the Spirit of truth with the worldly three-dimensional senses, nor with all the technical aids.

Today, one can read in generally available publications how short-lived the so-called state of science is today. To the extent that so-called technical progress develops, earlier generally accepted scientific findings are dismissed ever more quickly as "scientific error." Today, for example, the centuries-long held notion that the entire outer space is filled with a fine medium, a primordial substance, the so-called ether, which cannot be verified with human cognitive possibilities, is banned as a "scientific error."

But without this "ether," physically measurable phenomena such as the spreading of light waves in the seemingly empty outer space could not be explained, because the spreading of waves is not possible without a carrier substance.

According to Einstein and his theory of relativity, it was believed that it was possible to dispense with the assumption of such a primordial substance, the ether, in space. But already with the development of quantum physics, Einstein's theories were partially questioned again. And science is still searching in vain for the so-called universal formula, which should provide a plausible explanation for all the, until today, contradictory hypotheses of science. But new hypotheses merely raise ever new unresolved questions.

So today one is certain that almost four-fifths of the universe does not consist of visible matter, of the heavenly bodies visible to us, but of so-called dark matter that fills outer space and which seems dark to us.

However, science cannot directly prove dark matter experimentally, nor can it explain what this dark matter should consist of and why it should suddenly have emerged from a tiny particle out of nothing in a so-called Big Bang, as the current "Big Bang Theory" of science claims about the beginning of the universe.

Recently, a young physicist from John Hopkins University in the USA questioned this theory as well. Based on calculations, he pointed out the possibility that dark matter existed as a form of energy before the so-called Big Bang—but where does it come from?

Billions upon billions are spent by science to find answers to questions about the origin of life, which the Spirit of truth has at all times revealed long since to His human children through His prophets of God, and reveals it again today in all its detail.

But at all times there were also scientists who particularly recognized the limitations of their own world and thus, came to the realization of a higher power and the greatness of the Eternal Spirit and His creation. One of them is Max Planck, who received the Nobel Prize in Physics, and who is still highly regarded among scientists—and from whom the following words have been handed down:

"As a physicist, who for all his life served the down-to-earth science of investigating matter, I am certainly free of the suspicion of being considered a dreamer. And therefore, according to my experiences with the atom, I say the following:

There is no matter as such, all matter only comes into being and exists through a force, which brings the atomic particles into vibration and keeps them together in that tiny solar system of the atom. Since there exists neither an intelligent nor an eternal abstract power in the entire universe—humankind never succeeded to find the intensively longed for 'perpetuum mobile'—we have to assume a conscious, intelligent spirit behind this power.

This spirit is the primordial basis of all matter; not the visible, yet transitory matter is the real, the true—because matter would not exist at all without the spirit—but the invisible, immortal spirit is the true!

But since spirit cannot exist as such, and since every spirit belongs to a being, we have to assume, with compelling logic, spirit beings. But since

spirit beings also cannot be of themselves, but have to be created, therefore I do not fight shy to call this mysterious Creator in the very same way, as all peoples with culture on the Earth of earlier millennia have called him: 'God.'"
(http://www.worldreligiousportal.com/ forume/01/07_Articles/18_Tuebingen/ 0303018_Tuebingen.php)

The well-known mathematician, physicist and astronomer Karl Friedrich Gauss placed the salvation of the soul and the recognition of God above his scientific endeavors, in the following words:

"Besides this material world, another, a second, purely spiritual world order exists, with just as many diversities as that in which we live— much speaks for this, and we are to participate in it one day.

There are questions regarding which I would attach infinitely greater importance on the answers than mathematical ones, for example, about ethics, about our relationship to God, about our destiny and our future. There is for the soul the satisfaction of a higher kind, for that I do not need the material at all."

abriele continues writing:

Today it is comprehensively evident that everything is based on the Spirit, on the flowing, omnipresent, eternal Light-Ether. It is the All-Law, the bearer of consciousness of the inexhaustible energetic seas of light, seven times seven intensities of light of infinity.

I repeat: The flowing Spirit, the primordial eternal law, is the spiritually sustaining Being, also called light-ethereal carrier substance, also for all heavenly bodies of infinity.

The light-ethereal particles, light atoms upon light atoms, the Spirit, are in every particle, in every atom, and, as if automatically, orient themselves to every form of life, to every detail of life, whether fine-material, finer-material or coarse-material. Everything, but absolutely everything, receives according to the law of life: spirit of His Spirit.

Whether it is the divine beings that form a unity with the eternally flowing All-Law, the Spirit, whether it is the smallest—for us human beings the most inconspicuous spiritual species of life—every mineral, every plant species and animal form and every color nuance of infinity is given attention in the All-Law, the Spirit, which is the life.

It streams.
It draws.
It creates.
It gives.

So is it:
The All-Law is the All-giving, streaming, divine All-Life, which gives of itself via the All-communication, sending and receiving.

We human beings seek the eternal Spirit—and yet, He is present. We do not see Him—and yet, we are permeated by the Spirit, who is the All-life.

It is sad, very sad, when we think of our world, of the nations of the Earth. Hardly a person is content; everyone thinks and believes that he has to have more and that a proof has to be found for everything, also for the truth and the life. The best proof is each one of us, ourselves, if we orient ourselves according to the Ten Commandments of God and the teachings of Jesus of Nazareth. Then with time, we feel the omnipresence of life, the Spirit of truth, which is the love for God and neighbor.

Neither priests nor pastors are needed for this. No churches of stone, no baptism, no holy water, no ceremonies or the like are needed for this.

The only thing that makes us free and lets each one of us find our way to the truth is the Spirit of truth, who revealed Himself to the people of all the generations through prophets and prophetesses, through His divine messengers.

People complicate everything and ask questions after questions of the churches, also of the politicians and those powerful in economy and science.

The question can rightly be put to the conglomerate of state and church: From which spirit do they live, the holders of power, that is, the dogmatists?

What is the name of the hegemony that drives this system?

When the system administrators hear: *"The Spirit of truth, the Spirit of fusion, love of His love, the Eternal Kingdom,"* then many a one merely shrugs his shoulders indifferently and smiles, possibly pointing to the sacral divide of the institutional churches, which they serve with a consenting "nod."

The Eternal Kingdom cannot be fathomed with a "nod" and a belief in the church, and that is correct, since the Ten Commandments of God and the teachings of the Christ of God, once in Jesus of Nazareth, were, after all, rejected.

Strange—why, then, do people use His name and speak of "Christian values," and, at the same time, unabashedly engage in arms trade, just as the guild of priests carries its "unchristian" doings along on its banner, including the creed of their so-called "mystery of faith"?

The Eternal Kingdom, the principle of equality, unity, freedom and justice should not be brought into connection with this world, for it, after all, is the true life, the law of life, the love for God and neighbor.

As long as the so-called state powers of all nations are being drip-fed by the religions, nothing can thrive.

Since the separation of several divine beings from the Eternal Kingdom of truth, religious delusions exist, the shackling of believers, who have to live according to the demonic pattern of idolatry, and this, according to the demonic credo and under the supervision and control of the dictates from priests and the state.

People in all nations deliver themselves more and more to the signet, the dominion under the will of the demon.

In so-called "Christian countries," this hegemony is showing its effect, the well-known religious banner "these weapons come from Christian countries" is likewise showing its effect. Wouldn't it be more honest to affix straightaway the demonically appropriated trademark "from Christian countries" to all war equipment of the most diverse kinds? Perhaps this rating would have a corresponding success.

In order to keep up the appearances, one misuses the impeccable name of Jesus, the Christ, and perfidiously labels "from Christian countries."

It becomes a matter of course to claim worldwide that the Ten Commandments of God through Moses and the teachings of Jesus of Nazareth, His Sermon on the Mount, cannot be lived, with the result that then, in many nations of this Earth, a corresponding banner also waves: "under the hegemony of the demon."

At the same time, the banner also waves on the church steeples: "eternal punishment of hell," "eternal damnation" and in the core of the institutional churches, the altar requiem is called for: a mass for the dead, shortly before the downfall.

I know of no eternal Spirit that punishes and chastises, that instills in the believers an alleged eternal damnation as eternal punishment. The eternal Spirit blows where He wills, but a dictatorship of power is not in the All-Law of love for God and neighbor.

If, however, one rejects the eternal truth and deliberately invalidates it, then one cannot expect the true eternal God to support this disaster of world-cleaving arrogance.

Questions upon questions, explanations upon explanations.

What significance does religion have?

Erich Fromm, the founder of analytical social psychology, expressed this as follows:

It [religion, the church] has the task of preventing the psychological independence of the masses, of intellectually intimidating them, of bringing them into the socially necessary infantile submissiveness toward the rulers. (Erich Fromm, according to Hubertus Mynarek, "Papst-Entzauberung", pg. 43)

According to the German dictionary Duden, religion means: *faith, confession, doctrine of faith and denomination, as well as binding, religious orientation and belief.*

Religious means: *spiritual, ecclesiastical, sacred, not secular, theological or clerical.*

Religion also means: *devout in religion, strong in faith, believing, fearing God, orthodox, faithful, blessed, holy, pious, godly.*

However, all the listings of what religion means are irrelevant, because the Kingdom of

God, the Eternal Kingdom, is taking back the loan—the Light-Ether, which was given to the Fall-experts to take with them—in that the Eternal is transforming the density, dense matter, and gradually transforming it upward.

Religions are simply part of a certain solid materiality that exists since the Fall from the Kingdom of God.

In the end, they are a numerical mix that will dissolve together with all other common numerical combinations of the Fall. The numerical code, the numerical mix, is now under the action of the Light-Ether, which will dissolve, that is, transform, the density.

All matter is a Fall-disaster of the demon, which came about because he presumed to transform down the Light-Ether.

Anyone who still today—despite clarification—professes to the religious divide automatically professes to the rape of children and women, to war, manslaughter and murder, torture and cruelty.

The question is: Was there ever anything based on religion other than these grievous and bloody chapters?

Bertrand Russell, philosopher, writer and mathematician, formulated it in his time as follows:

It is possible that mankind is on the threshold of a golden age; but, if so, it will be necessary first to slay the dragon that guards the door, and this dragon is religion.
(https://www.brainyquote.com/quotes/bertrand_russell_402130)

People in the spirit of the love of neighbor fulfill what is righteous before God: the Ten Commandments of God through Moses and the teachings of peaceableness of Jesus of Nazareth.

The wind of yesterday has only a few frozen images left for today, which are wafted by the grace of the true God, so that yesterday serves as an admonishment, because the Fall-authority has lost.

The demonic scepter, with which the hegemony of suffering, murder and exploitation was carried over the Earth for generations upon generations, has brought about its own downfall.

The renovation of the universes is in progress, for the New Age wants to rise, the Age of the Lily, Sophia, the Wisdom of God with the Christ of God, for a free and more light-filled time.

In this spirit, the Christ of God is active, for wherever two or three are gathered in His name, His Spirit, the Spirit of truth, is among them.

We will be glad to send you
our current catalog of books, CDs and DVDs,
as well as free excerpts on many different topics

Gabriele Publishing House – The Word
P.O. Box 2221, Deering, NH 03244, USA
North America: Toll-Free No. 1-844-576-0937
International Orders: 49-9391-504-843
www.Gabriele-Publishing-House.com